THE WORLD ACCORDING TO KYLIE:

This tale tells the story of a young but ambitious reporter named Kylie.

Kylie is the oldest kid of Mr. & Mrs. Snoops, the richest family in Sumpkinville. She has three stinky brothers: Noah, Bobby, and Dustin.

Now, some people say that although Kylie is a very smart and pretty girl, she can be noisy, a bit weird, and if they are being honest, perhaps sometimes even a drama queen.

But never did the folks in Sumpkinville believe that it's Kylie's first day as the youngest reporter at the Grumbling Ogre Times, and Mr. Ogre has a spectacular assignment for her.

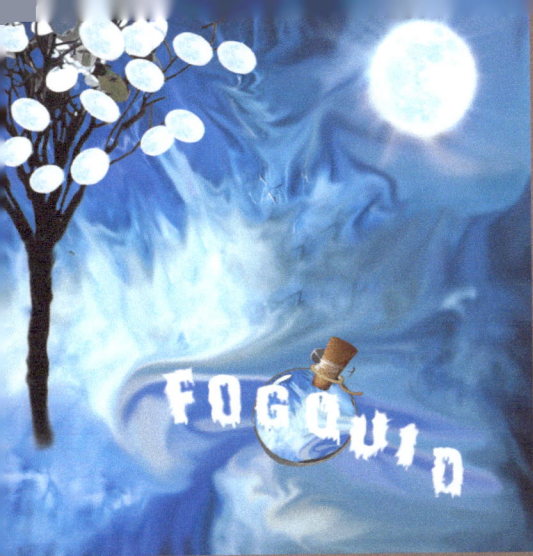

"Good Morning, Kylie, the scoop this morning is that Pepperz Pumpkin Patch has an exciting new addition to the pumpkin patch. Can you go and check it out?

NEWS

THE GRUMBLING OGRE

founded 1953

GIANT PUMPKIN LARGER THAN THE SNOOPS MANSION

Sir Pepper has shared exclusively the most exciting news with the grumbling Ogre! The patch has just hatched a giant blue pumpkin. Now, this pumpkin isn't just huge; apparently, once daily it vomits rainbow glitter, which then turns into rainbow cats!!!!!! How did this happen? Well, the rumor is that scientists recently have spotted a comet called Aarion in our atmosphere. Could this pumpkin be as a result of a future calamity between the human race and alien civilization's ? Or could these rainbow cats be aliens themselves?

goods on system applies. Finansial news new year. Finansial account opens all over the world.

opens all over the world.

NEWS

THE GRUMBLING OGRE

NO FAKE NEWS

founded 1953

CAT FOOD SOLD OUT!!!!!!!!!

The town of Sumpkinville has run out of cat food, and apparently everyone is trying to feed rainbow cats.

goods on | system applies. Finansial news

new year. Finansial account opens all over the world.

opens all over the world.

The following day, Mr. Ogre calls Kylie to his office.
"Kylie, here at the Grumbling Ogre, we tell the truth.
We simply cannot tolerate FAKE NEWS because liars never get anywhere in life.

Since your article was published, citizens wasted money on cat food and spent all day looking for rainbow cats!!!
This is just not the way things are done,"
counsels Mr. Ogre.

NEWS

THE GRUMBLING OGRE

founded 1953

NOT SO GIANT

Sorry

PUMPKIN AFTER ALL

Citizens Grumbling regrets to report that the Giant pumpkin wasn't so giant after all. The truth is that it's actually no bigger than a car.   In addition, Sir Pepper shared that he contributes this large pumpkin to his newest fertilizer, Growmania. This new formula, complete with unicorn hair, is also thought to be the cause of the vomiting glitter the pumpkin is experiencing. NO ALIEN WORRIES SUMPKINVILLE IS SAFE. The Grumbling Ogre is truly sorry for any inconvenience this article has caused.

goods on system applies. Finansial news new year. Finansial account opens all over the world.

opens all over the world.

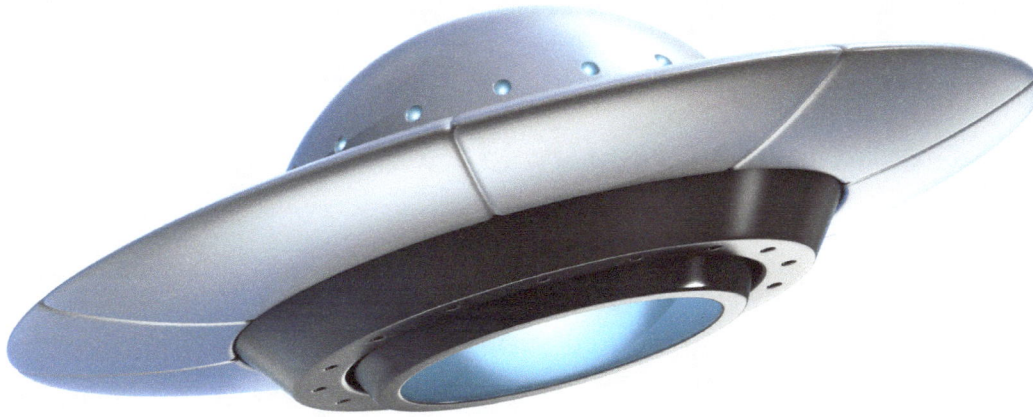

The next day, Mr. Ogre decides to give Kylie one more chance. "I received a phone call from Professor D this morning. Apparently, he has bred a remarkable new animal. Can you go over and check it out?" asks Mr. Ogre.

"I am on it," replies Kylie. "Kylie, keep your story real. Remember, no FAKE NEWS," says Mr. Ogre in a stern voice.

"I will, Mr. Ogre," promises Kylie.

NEWS

THE GRUMBLING OGRE

NO FAKE NEWS

founded 1953

ATHENA AND POSEIDON'S LOVE CHILD IS BORN

The Sumpkinville Zoo is hosting a remarkable Pegallamsus, which is believed to be the child of Athena and Poseidon. This creature, which is part Llama and Pegasus, is not only beautiful, but can also grant wishes and speak 15 different languages.

goods on system applies. Finansial news new year. Finansial account opens all over the world.

news

opens all over the world.

NEWS

THE GRUMBLING OGRE

NO FAKE NEWS

founded 1953

INSANE RAIN CAUSES FLOODING - WHY IS POSEIDON ANGRY AT US?

The town of Sumpkinville is experiencing huge amounts of rain, causing all the streets of Sumpkinville to flood. Residents are wondering what has angered Poseidon.

UNICORNS AND PEGASUS BATTLE IN THE BANK

Yesterday, for reasons unknown, a unicorn and a Pegasus battled inside the Sumpkinville bank, literally destroying the inside of the bank.
No worries, though the ATMs are working…

A frustrated Mr. Ogre calls Kylie into his office first thing. "KYLIE, YOU HAVE ANGERED THE GODS!! AND CAUSED A BATTLE BETWEEN UNICORNS AND PEGASUS!!!!!

Your exaggerations MUST STOP!!!!!"

"What?" asks Kylie who stood in shock.

"I have angered the GODS???? I am so sorry, Mr. Ogre, what should I do?"

"JUST TELL THE TRUTH, KYLIE.

A GOOD REPORTER ALWAYS TELLS THE TRUTH."

NEWS

THE GRUMBLING OGRE

founded 1953

REALLY

Sorry

IT MUST HAVE BEEN LOVE, BUT IT'S OVER NOW

NEWS

THE GRUMBLING OGRE

NO FAKE NEWS

founded 1953

Well, folks, it appears that Athena and Poseidon are not actually the parents of Sumpkinville's newest animal, the Pegallamasus.

It was actually created in Professor D's classroom over at the V.V.A. (Vladimir Vizard Academy).

Professor D donated this animal to the Sumpkinville Zoo. Again, the Grumbling Ogre apologizes for this mistake and will donate $10,000.00 to the zoo for this unfortunate

goods on   system applies. Finansial news   new year. Finansial account opens all over the world.
news   opens all over the world.

Kylie this isyour last chance famous rapper, Oliver "Fish Bowl" Montgomery, is coming to Sumpkinville. Go and cover the story!

NEWS

THE GRUMBLING OGRE

NO FAKE NEWS

founded 1953

FISH BOWL TO HOST FREE CONCERT AT ROLLING OAKS MALL

Oliver Montgomery, AKA as Fish Bowl, just released his latest album titled Fish Wars. Within hours of it release, the album went gold.

In an effort to give back to Sumpkinville, Oliver has agreed to host a free concert on Friday at 9:00 PM at Rolling Oaks Mall.

ational goods on   system applies. Finansial news   new year. Finansial account opens all over the world.

NEWS

THE GRUMBLING OGRE

NO FAKE NEWS

founded 1953

COMPLIANCE DEPARTMENT CLOSES
MALL FOR OCCUPENCY VIOLATION

It appears that the entire town of Sumpkinville went to the mall yesterday looking to get free tickets for Oliver's "Free" concert.

We're CLOSED

system applies. Finansial news

new year. Finansial account opens all over the world.

opens all over the world.

"Kylie, it appears that we have another problem," states Mr. Ogre who appears to be very angry. "What do you mean?" asks Kylie.

The Rolling Oaks mall had to close down yesterday because of the article you wrote. Mr. Ogre handed Kylie the article she wrote; as she read it, she giggled. "Kylie, you cannot keep publishing lies," says Mr. Ogre and then went on to say "Due to the mall closing,

The Grumbling Orge will now host a free concert at considerable cost!"

NEWS

THE GRUMBLING OGRE

founded 1953

REALLY REALLY

Sorry

national goods on system applies. Finansial news new year. Finansial account opens all over the world.

sial news

account opens all over the world.

NEWS

THE GRUMBLING OGRE

NO FAKE NEWS

founded 1953

THE GRUMBLING OGRE MAKES UP FOR ITS MISTAKES

After the chaos caused by our article, the Grumbling Ogre has agreed to host a free concert. Come and See Fishbowl perform at Rolling Oaks Mall. Log on to www.grumblingogre.com and select free tickets.

goods on system applies. Finansial news new year. Finansial account opens all over the world. news opens all over the world.

After the concert, Kylie lay in bed, so exhausted that she quickly fell asleep. While she slept, she dreamed about rainbows and unicorns, but her dream quickly became a nighmare.

Suddenly, Kylie found herself in a dark foggy place, being chased by miniature rainbow cats! Next, she heard fluttering wings and then owls and an angry Pegallamasus! Behind the Pegallamasus tridents flew through the air.
She ran inside a door that seemed familiar to her. It was the newspaper where she worked, and she gasped when she saw a sign on the door that said closed! Kylie screamed "NOOOOOOOO" and then woke up.

Once she realized it was just a dream, she thought to herself "I will NEVER exaggerate again, lies come back to haunt you, Mr. Ogre was right."

We're CLOSED

Founded 1953

NEWS

THE GRUMBLING OGRE

NO FAKE NEWS

founded 1953

KYLIE'S APOLOGY

Dear Sumpkinville,

I am extremely sorry for all my exaggerated articles. I have lied to all of you, and because of it, Rolling Oaks Mall had to close. I angered the Greek gods, which caused the bank to be destroyed and much more. But I promise that I have learned my lesson, and learned from my mistakes. From now on, I will ALWAYS tell the truth.

Sincerely,

Kylie Reed Snoops

Contributing Authors & Characters

Ashlyn LaQue

Ashlyn LaQue an eleven year old who aspires to be a pediatrician when she grows up. She is a loving and outgoing girl who enjoys reading, drawing and gymnastics. Ashlyn enjoys spending time with her family on vacation and loves her dog Chloe.

Annabell Knox

Annabell Knox is eleven years old and wants to be a gamer when she grows up. She enjoys playing Fortnite, drawing and loves horses. Annabell is a fun loving, imaginative person who loves to make people laugh.

Blyss Byrnes

Blyss Loves drawing, reading, and swimming. She wants to be a book illustrator when she grows up. She's an artist, and she's a great big sister and daughter.

ALLEGRA BYRNES

Allegra loves nature, animals and babies. She is a great swimmer, and she wants to be a biologist when she grows up. She loves learning about animals and plants and she enjoys being outdoors.

VICTORIA STAMPS

I am Victoria and I am eight years old. I am kind, nice and thankful. I speak Hebrew, and once I broke my arm, if you look at my left arm you will see two scars from the metal pins the doctor put in my arm.

SOFIA I. MELCHOR

Sofia I. Melchor is twelve years old and attends Eleanor Kolitz Hebrew Language Academy. She enjoys listening to Hamilton, reading Percy Jackson, and drawing. She hopes to either become an artist, a pharmacist or a pilot.

Katrin Stamps

Katrin goes to Eleanor Kolitz Hebrew Language Academy. She likes to draw, Harry Potter and is obsessed with the show Stranger Things. She is twelve years old and likes pop, and rock music.

Kiesten O. Puente

Kiesten O. Puente is eleven years old and has a love for reading. She has been awarded the Royal Top Reader award from Idea South Flores. When she grows up she wants to be a research scientist so she can cure diseases. Kiersten has a quick wit, enjoys spending time with her family, friends, and her cats. She also enjoys writing and listening to music.

Ella Mayzel

Ella Mayzel is nine years old,
she likes to ride
horses, swim and play soccer.
She wants to be an artist when
she grows up. Ella has a sweet
heart and loves to help others.

Chloe Mayzel

Chloe Mayzel is twelve years old.
She likes horseback
riding and reading.
Her favorite color is blue and she
loves pop music. Chloe
attends Eleanor Kolitz
Hebrew Language Academy.

Sumpkinville Characters

Ella Mayzel is nine years old, she likes to ride horses, swim and play soccer. She wants to be an artist when she grows up. Ella has a sweet heart and loves to help others.

Ella Mayzel

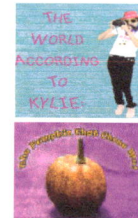

Nathan Kyle Treviño is 12 years old and aspires to become a therapist when he grows up. He embraces life, makes friends wherever he goes and continues to wear his heart on his sleeve.

Nathan Kyle Trevino

I am Victoria and I am eight years old. I am kind, nice and thankful. I speak Hebrew, and once I broke my arm, if you look at my left arm you will see two scars from the metal pins the doctor put in my arm.

Victoria Stamps

Kiesten O. Puente is eleven years old and has a love for reading. She has been awarded the Royal Top Reader award from Idea South Flores. When she grows up she wants to be a research scientist so she can cure diseases. Kiersten has a quick wit, enjoys spending time with her family, friends, and her cats. She also enjoys writing and listening to music.

Kiesten O. Puente

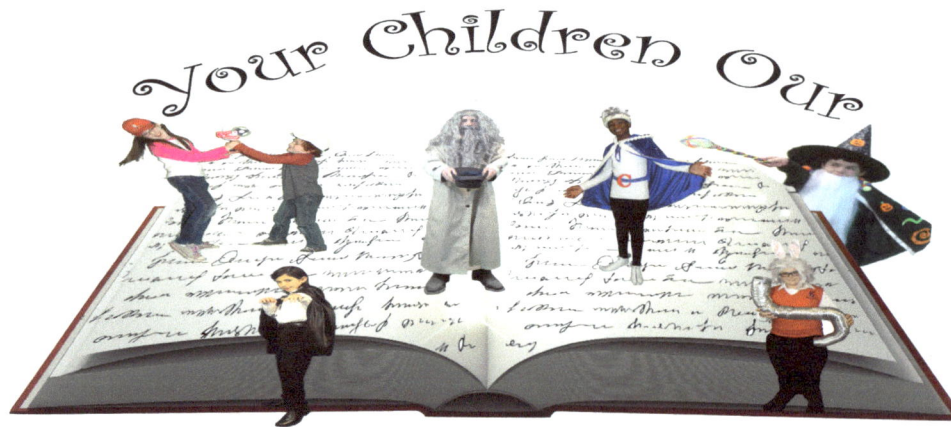

Your Children Our Stories

CSB INNOVATIONS

www.csbinnovations.com

www.ingramcontent.com/pod-product-compliance
Lightning Source LLC
Chambersburg PA
CBHW040404100426

42811CB00017B/1826